QUEEN OF SPADES

CONNECTING TO TRADITIONAL AFRICAN AMERICAN CONJURE & DIVINATION

BY
QUEEN CO.MEADOWS,
THE HOODOO QUEEN™

QUEEN OF SPADES

Connecting to Traditional African American Conjure & Divination

Content: Queen Co. Meadows, Sasha Ravae
Cover/Art Design: Conjure South Publications
Editors: Queen Co. Meadows and Sasha Ravae

Published by:
Conjure South Publications
P.O. Box 404
Mobile, AL 36601
www.ConjureSouth.com

TABLE OF CONTENTS

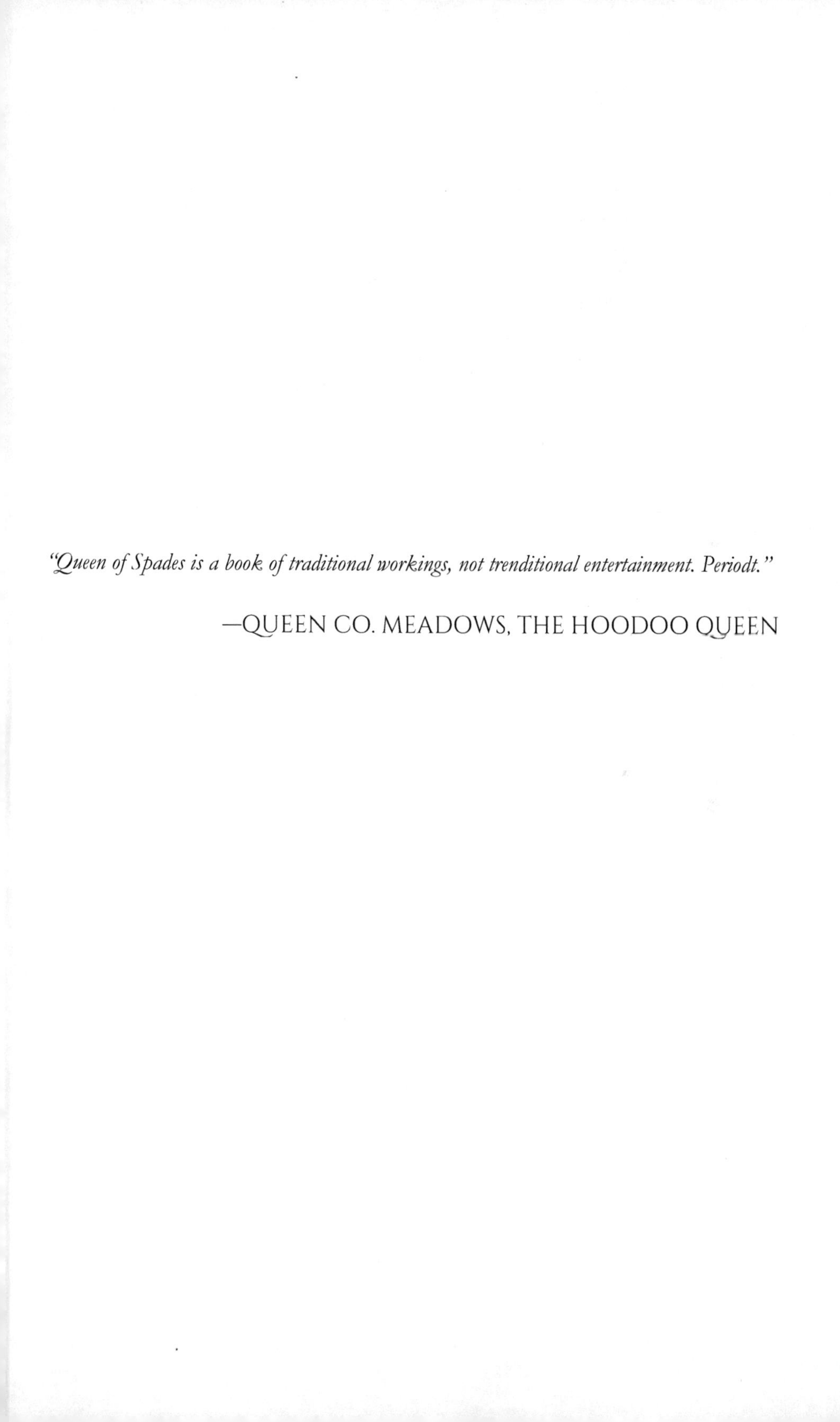

"Queen of Spades is a book of traditional workings, not trenditional entertainment. Periodt."

—QUEEN CO. MEADOWS, THE HOODOO QUEEN

DISCLAIMER:

This book is an educational piece of literature that will allow anyone to practice the method of conjure as well as root work. It is very important to me, not as the author, but as a spiritual leader, to communicate the importance of education, and not just the magic and the how-to.

Everyone has the ability to practice magic, but it's important to gain respect for that system first. Another space is to gain knowledge you can use to recognize if something has been done to you or a family member. By doing that, you are honoring the ancestors, elders, and the descendants of that lineage. What you want to do personally is on you, because anyone has the ability to practice whatever they want.

This is an ancestral-based system. This is a cultural system; therefore, the biggest, boldest, clearest line that should not be crossed is the line of authority. Do not take this book as a guide to teach others. This is for you to connect with *your* self-empowerment, but this does not give you the authority to speak for the ancestors, elders, or descendants.

Also, please, understand that within this book, I will be using English and French terms, or *Franglish,* because it's my lineage, and it's how my family speaks when referring to products.

ANCESTOR DEDICATION

First and foremost, I have to give the highest form of recognition and honor to the ancestors who came before us, regarding who we are as people and where our magic comes from. It is important for me to give thanks to them because they are our foundation. Due to this, I need the ancestors to know my gratitude for the strength that they possessed through their trials. I thank them for their wisdom, wit, and esoteric knowledge of the unknown during their trials. I thank them for the medicine that they provided. I give that appreciation because it is the roots that sprout multiple branches in our lives as African Americans, or people of color. I mean for the mundane *and* the magic, the spirit and the earthly, I have to thank them.

Because, through them, we also possess these powers, and we're able to be root workers, artists, etc. I thank them for all that they are, all they ever were, and all that they will ever be.

Understanding that the asè they possess and the asè that they used to be victorious are the same vibrations, frequencies, and blood that flows through my veins. Without them, there is no me. Without me, there is no them, and I thank them for their everlasting love.

I thank my ancestors for designing me to be the successor of my lineage. I also would like to thank my spirit guides who protect the roads that I travel.

I think we all should be able to thank our ancestors for allowing us to be a part of them. It is something that is absolutely incredible. Think about the world right now; our people have dealt with all of the horrors of slavery, but we are still here, still standing. That is a clear indication that nothing can stop you if you know *who* you are.

Through your ancestors, you can truly know your power.

AUTHOR'S ACKNOWLEDGEMENTS

I first would like to acknowledge my ancestors, because, again, without them, I wouldn't've been able to fulfill my purpose in creating a platform that allows me to connect our people to themselves.

I also have to give thanks to my living elders, who groomed me into the Queen of our family's spiritual lineage. I thank them for their encouragement and their stamp of approval. I am fulfilled in my heart knowing that I am making my elders and ancestors proud.

I am also thankful for my partner for being a very vital part of my business, providing the extra hands that allow things to run smoothly, in addition to wanting me to succeed even beyond my own imagination. It is so beautiful, and it really touches me. I understand the sacrifices that my other half has made because of the love that he possesses for me. Even though he may not understand why I do what I do—my spiritual purpose—he's been beyond supportive without any hesitation, which allows the success of our platform to excel.

I want to give thanks to Black Eden Publications for their energy, wisdom, and knowledge. Thank you for seeing enough value in what I'm doing to dedicate your time, because time is the most precious thing we have.

TERMINOLOGY

Here are some common terms that you need to know prior to reading this book. Please, make sure that you take the time to review these terms so that you can have a better understanding of the text as you move forward.

Anointed: To use oils on an item

Bindin': To restrict someone or tie something up

Broom: A spiritual tool that is used

Cologne/Waters (Ex. Florida Water): Can be used for cleansing

Condition: A problem

Conjure/Hoodoo Oils: Oils that are meant to anoint your objects

Conjure: Magic from any ethnic background, not just Hoodoo. Umbrella term for magic.

Container Work: Any spell work that allows you to contain something, using jars, a box, a bottle, a locket, or a charm. Any object that you can place items in and seal.

Crossin' (or *Being Crossed*): To be spelled. A harmful spell has been done to you.

Dirt: The mixing of herbs, roots, and consecrated dirt for spell work and to lay tricks.

Divination: A method of gaining divine insight and clarity on situations, utilizing tarot cards, bones, playing cards, waters, elements, etc.

Doin' Work: The action of spell crafting or conjuring. That also goes into 2 different spaces: rituals and work.

Fixin' (or *Fix*): The preparation of an item for a person that was anointed or dressed. Once it's been conjured, it's fixed.

Floor Washes: An herbal mixture that is created to wash the sidewalk in front of your home.

Foot Track: Using people's footprints or using their path

Gifted/Born with a Gift: An individual who is born with spiritual abilities in the African American community, a conjurer of Hoodoo, a seer, a healer, a root worker.

Hoodoo: African American Conjure (I will be speaking from my lineage—African American conjure, Hoodoo (more inland conjure), Obeah (a West Indian conjure), and Gris-gris (cove conjure found in the gulf coast). These are all forms of magic.

Incense: Resin, roots, leaves, anything that can make a smoke

Jinx: A workin' that is done to affect luck

Layin' Tricks: Laying something down in someone's path

Lights: Candles (can be used to attract or repel as a spiritual element)

Mojo (Bag/Hand): A Hoodoo amulet that contains a spirit that is carried on you or inside your home. They carry herbs, roots, bones, or whatever the spiritual worker decides.

Nature: Someone's genitals

Perfume: A sweet fragrance used for blessings

Personal Concern: An item belonging to a person—hair, something physically from their body, or an item

Petitions: Your prayers, your desires written on a piece of paper or on an item

Powder: Used in food and spaces that may be more difficult to conceal

Practitioner: Uses spiritual tools and supplies to assist them in their life, but they don't work for people.

Ritual: A deeper, more intense commitment in your conjuring. It involves deeper knowledge and is quite esoteric in its approach.

Root Work: Traditionally, a root worker was an African American man or woman who was an herbalist. They brought knowledge from Africa on how to work with roots.

Roots: Actual roots to be used in a traditional root worker/medicinal sense, or a term of reflecting magic. (Traditionally, it was not used as that term.)

Smoking: African American incense—using roots, resins, and leaves to create a smoke. (We did not smudge.)

Spiritual Baths: Herbal mixtures that you would bathe in, in a spiritual sense.

Spiritual Worker: A person who is gifted in Hoodoo or African conjure, who possesses magic to work for the people; an anointed person.

Stuff/Doin' Stuff: They know spell work, they know magic, they know Hoodoo.

Sweetenin': Making a situation better by using herbs

Throwin': Deliberately targeting someone

Tricks: Spelling someone without them knowing it

Uncrossing: To uncross a condition

Work: A very general term, but 'work' also can mean that you are actually in the process of conjuring your desire.

PREFACE

WHAT IS THIS BOOK ABOUT?

Queen of Spades is the medium that connects the descendants of enslaved Africans to their traditional spirituality, their magic, and the customs of their people.

This is traditional African American conjure, best known as Hoodoo, coming directly from its descendants, from a family that is known throughout the Americas and West Indies, documented since we have been enslaved in the western hemisphere.

This book will give the descendants of these people a look into who we were *before* slavery. With recipes to reshape the present reality, this book gives you the tools to gain clarity and the answers needed for the darkness in your life. This book is true encouragement from your ancestors.

This book is the conduit, the medium, the connection, and introduction to your ancestors. This is a book that you can use to look into your great-great-great-great grandmother or grandfather's eyes and have a conversation with them as they guide you. It gives you the ammunition that you were designed to walk with.

Being that I was brought up by people from the 1900s, I am bringing you the *true* version of Hoodoo, not a mix of mess and magic. We're not doing that. This is not glitter and unicorns; this is *traditional* Hoodoo. This is giving you the different forms of divination that we would have used in the past that may resonate with you now. This is the first door that you must open in order to understand *your* magic.

This is a book that will identify what Hoodoo actually is—a magical gift, *not* a magical tool. This is meant to present Hoodoo as magic, not as a healing or divination modality, and bring dignity and structure to what Hoodoo truly is.

Queen of Spades is the *truth* of Hoodoo.

HOW TO USE THIS BOOK

Queen of Spades allows you to understand the different variables of Hoodoo—how to cleanse yourself, attract love and more favor, and become luckier, as well as how to spiritually heal your body and spaces. This book will provide you with a solid foundation no matter your spiritual preference. This is that next step.

GENERAL HISTORY

As people of color, we have complained and cried about our spiritual narrative being stolen from us and then being *sold* to us by non-people-of-color, but those days are over! I can no longer allow Hoodoo, which is *not* a secondary spirituality to us, to be misrepresented. In regard to African spiritual systems, Hoodoo was our go-to; it wasn't Christianity.

I am convicted to bring respect back to the African American spiritual community and back to our elders. I, as Queen Co. Meadows, the Hoodoo Queen, the Dark Mother, I cannot allow the disrespect of our elders, of my ancestors, or of other people's ancestors to go on any longer.

There is absolutely nothing wrong with giving respect to a culture or a group of people as who they are.

CHAPTER 1
People of Earth & Blood— the History of Our People & Our Magic

WHO ARE WE?

To start off, who were we before we became enslaved Africans? We were the people of earth.

This means that we understood the value of the earth, being a part of earth, and our responsibility to her. We understood the spirit of the elements and provided gratitude for that. We were people of blood.

During slavery, some people who were enslaved were wood workers, blacksmiths, farmers, midwives, and traditional doctors. Some people came as conjurers, seers, and possessed the gifts of magic. Our magic is our purpose on this earth.

Our people also understood that those who possess the gift of magic have the ability to shift reality in current situations. Those who couldn't had to look for religious solutions.

When you're honoring the river, the air, or the wind, you find that our gods, goddesses, and spirits are tied with those aspects as well. In the elements, we can find ourselves.

For example, if I possess the gift of conjure, and I'm in a space of fire, my spiritual work will have to do with fire. The same if I lived near a river, then I would be in a space of water.

Getting into the space of understanding, no matter if it was the Yoruba people, or the Congo people, or Togo, or whatever country, we understood those religions, but we also understood magic.

Our magic is not our religion. Magic is its own entity. The reason why our people did not mix magic with religion (the Orisa or Lwa) was because they had responsibilities, guidelines, rules, shrines, and acknowledgments of those deities. Magically, there is no God. There was no shrine. We didn't have altars in our magic; that was never a thing. It didn't start to become popular until the 1980s or 90s.

Understanding that space, our people are from West Africa—Yoruba, Nigeria, Senegal, Ghana. The Congo, Benin, and Togo are places that our magic came from; it looked different in Africa than it did in the western hemisphere.

For example, there was no such thing as a Voodoo/Hoodoo doll, but there were nkisi, which held a spirit to bring healing and expose the truth, not to bring harm.

The nails that are present were not for pain, but were representations of promises, but that changed because of our experiences. Our magic and religion changed.

In Haitian Voodoo, Lwa, there are warriors, fighters, but none of those spirits exist in Vodun. Again, this is due to our experience. Religion is not magic. It is a way of life.

Our ancestors are the foundation of our magic, of our religion, in the African diaspora. Some of us are the descendants of the gods and the goddesses that we serve. We are the descendants of the people who carried magic in their blood. However, let me make this clear, Hoodoo is not a religion. It is a magical system, a magical ability.

WHAT IS HOODOO?

Hoodoo is the African American Conjure that stems from our African religions and African magic, like Guinea Guinea, Juju, Gris-gris, and our experience as enslaved Africans through the transatlantic trade route.

WHAT DOES THAT MEAN?

We may have used the color red for our mojo bags because it was the color of the god of protection. It was a space for our African magic. This means that we understood that a woman's menstrual blood held healing and compelling powers. Understanding those things comes from our African magic. The biggest thing that makes Hoodoo African is our enslaved African experience. The rape and trauma, the stealing of our spirit and culture, the killing of men and women, the separation of our tribes in America, the lights vs. darks, the big from the small, a certain texture of hair vs. another, making you believe that your god abandoned you, this is why it is African. This is why Hoodoo is African. This is why it is okay for it to be exclusive because a non-person-of-color who is not from the African diaspora, they can sympathize with our trauma, but they cannot *empathize* with the asè that was born out of that trauma.

"You can learn the method, but you cannot learn my asè."

WHAT HOODOO IS NOT

Hoodoo is not American conjure! It is not a big mix of African, Native, and European magic that makes a big beautiful system. This is a lie that has been told, another narrative that has been repeated so many times by so many appropriators because they have more influence, and people believe them.

Let's be clear, when we hear people say that African American conjure was influenced by this culture, by that culture, or by this group of people, what is the truth?

We, as black people, being owned by other races of people, recognized that other cultures had traditions too, and we observed as many as we could.

It was once told to me that Hoodoo was influenced by the Jews because they used oil lamps. Lamps were in all the aboriginal places. Traditionally, we didn't use kerosene lamps. We used other variations. However, kerosene lamps were assessible, so we used the tools that were accessible to us at the time.

Hoodoo is not the second-hand version or a step down from other African spiritual systems. In the Southeast of the United States of America, it was our go-to. We knew to go to the stones, roots, and herbs, because our religion was taken from us. Hoodoo is not a watered-down version of any spiritual system, and it's not a weaker form of magic. It's our first system as enslaved African people, and it's not to be confused with New Orleans Voodoo. And, we're ending with that statement there because that is a *whole* other book. Period.

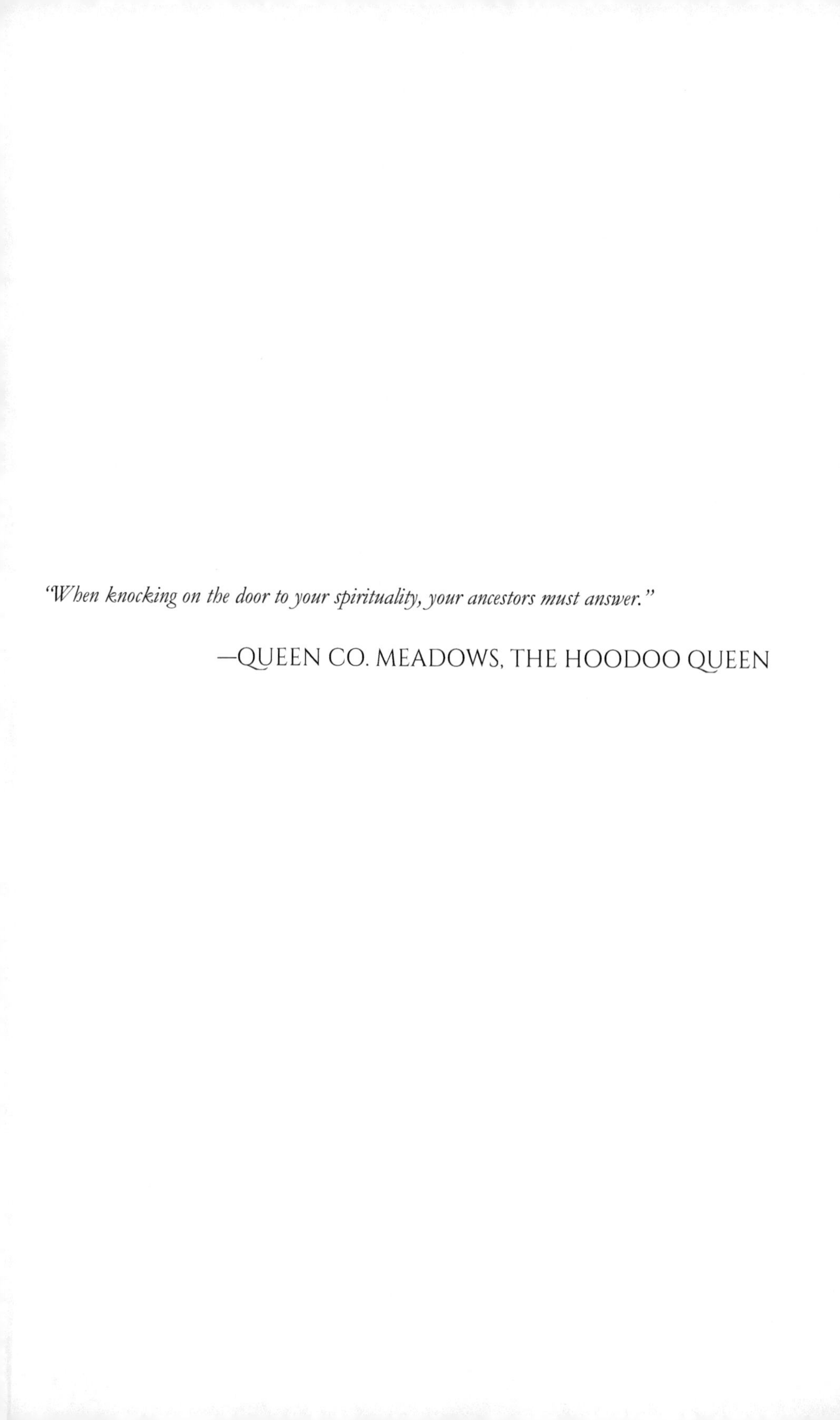

"When knocking on the door to your spirituality, your ancestors must answer."

—QUEEN CO. MEADOWS, THE HOODOO QUEEN

CHAPTER 2

Ancestral Altars & Communication—the Start to Your Spiritual Experience Before Spell Work

We begin this space, as I have done this entire time, by honoring the ancestors. Our spirituality from religion to magic begins with our ancestors. You find this very clear through ancestor spaces.

Through those spaces, you give them honor and reverence. You see that I didn't say "altar." Altars were not a thing in our tradition.

It's important to know who the ancestors are. Individuals you know or could have known are your blood lineage: your family members, those who are recognized through your blood DNA. In the space of reverence, you can also look at your ancestral court lineage: those you have picked up along the way.

Even our religions are ancestral-based. This is where people get mad at African spirituality because our gods were our ancestors.

UNDERSTANDING WHO THEY ARE

The next space is understanding the purpose of the ancestor—to protect and to guide. Understand that their protection may show up as rejection or delay sometimes, but this is guiding you onto a better path. So, give the ancestors thanks for all that they are.

Let's say that you need direction on getting a good job, for example. You fill out 50 applications and get rejected 49 times. That rejection was meant to protect you. There is always a purpose for delays.

Understand that the ancestors are nothing without you, and you are nothing without them. So, the less you do for them, the more confused your life will be.

Social media outlets, such as YouTube, Facebook, MyBook, Twitter, Twatter, say that the ancestors are going to come to you in your dreams. But this is not the only way that they can connect, so make sure that you've done your due diligence by looking into various methods. Cards, oracles, bones, angel numbers, smells, scents, feelings, or even just your intuition, make sure you know what medium works for you.

Also, it's very important to build your spiritual vocabulary. My ancestors speak to me differently than yours do you. THIS IS WHAT YOU

AND *YOUR* FAMILY DO…this is not traditional. For example, blue butterflies in my family represent a baby boy being born. This is the spiritual vocabulary that was passed down to us.

As you're connecting with your own ancestral lineage, a blue butterfly in your family may mean that a male dies. Becoming aware of these types of signs and symbols is how you build your vocabulary.

Developing your ancestral reverence, communication, and relationship is not a spiritual ability; it's an experience. Everyone has the ability to access that guidance and protection. Whether we all decide to listen to it is another story.

Honoring is not magic; it's not Hoodoo. This is a custom of our people—Obeah, Gris-gris, Ifá, Santería, etc. Reverence looks different depending on the religion.

An ancestral space along your spiritual journey is practical and simple. There are only two items you need to begin and two items to end—a candle and a glass of water.

The trends tell you that you need a white tablecloth, Florida Water, money, food, crystals, incense, nine glasses of water, and a Bible, but this is not true. None of the enslaved people had access to these sorts of things at the time.

Because we had to conceal what we did, our ancestral space looked very different. Maybe, it was a fire pit, and you would pour out a little water as a libation. As time went on, all you needed was a glass of water and a candle. You may have just used items instead of pictures.

White tablecloths, white flowers—this comes from a particular African religion—this was how you gave honor to the ancestors.

When you're in a religion, it requires specific things, certain responsibilities; where, magic is practical and simple. If you have fire and water, you can connect with your ancestors.

While this could be talked about for multiple books, I actually have an ancestral altar online course that explains all the do's and don'ts when it comes to setting up your ancestral space. Find out more now at: www.conjuresouth.com.

With that being said, in order to start your magic, you need to honor your actual ancestral DNA. Don't just pull people, ideas, or deities that do not honor your ancestral lineage. If any people are still alive in the photos, do not use their picture. Remember, the dead come for the dead.

Also, do not set up your ancestral space in your bedroom. Your grandma doesn't want to see you bump and grind in the name of love with nobody. And, the last thing is you do not have to have your candle burning all day. You can dedicate just 10-minutes, and that's enough.

CHAPTER 3
Hoodoo Cleansing

WHAT IS A CLEANSING?

A cleansing is the action, the initiative, or responsibility to remove whatever is holding you down, binding you, tying you, or anything else. This space of removing gives you the ability to release or remove negative intentions that you are personally holding on to and projecting or having projected onto you.

There are multiple levels to cleansing within the tradition, as well as African American folk practices. Cleansing stretches across the board in many ways.

Many believe it to be only baths, but there are levels to this ish. A bath may work for you, while a candle may work for others.

What Does Cleansing in Hoodoo Look Like, Smell Like, Feel Like?

Understanding that cleansing is the ability to remove what is stopping or delaying you from receiving the blessings that you should be receiving. These setbacks or restrictions may be projected onto you by yourself or by someone else. Either way, they need to be removed. It is the first step. It puts you in the space to receive your blessings.

Cleansings can be done on particular spaces in your home or land, at your job, or another professional location. Understand that cleansing comes in many different ways.

Cleansings can be seen as a removal; it can be a banishing, it can be block buster, or a road opener. From that space, it can come from any elemental source—fire, water, air, or earth.

For example, when grounding, or walking around barefoot, you are giving into the earth, so something will be given back to you. This is a space of symbiotic relationships. You then have water. You can use this elemental space by giving to the river and putting your feet in the water.

WHICH ONE DO I USE?

I always say go with your birth element. This is your natural element, but this is something that we have to understand—we are made from many different elements. For example, you may be under an earth sign, but your moon sign could be fire, and your rising could be air. If earth is your first element, you could look into different herbs to use, for example. If that doesn't help you, try cleansing with another element. It's all about the process of elimination.

You never want to say, "I feel worse than when I went in."

All of this can be done through any element that has the ability to cleanse you. When it comes to Hoodoo, fire and candles are used to remove things. Water, baths and oils, basically anything liquid, can also be used. Air and smoking are used to remove things too. Remember, we don't use "smudge." And, when it comes to earth, brushing is used to remove things.

One thing that's important to know before we get into the cleansing work is you have to be ready to be cleansed. It's going to remove things that *need* to be removed from your life—that may be your husband, that raggedy job, or even that bad Party City wig. Now, you may not want to, but you *need* to.

When it comes to being ready to be cleansed, it is important to know that it is going to create a space of vulnerability.

Ask yourself, "Is my space conducive with what I'm trying to receive?"

Like I always say, "a cluttered closet cannot have new things." You can't claim or release because there are things in the way. Until we release our personal restraints, we cannot release our external restraints.

Cleansing needs to be done periodically. That can be daily, weekly, monthly, seasonally, and even annually. And, it can look different for everyone.

For example, a daily cleanse can include grounding; weekly, a bath; monthly, a smoking or steam ritual, and annually may be all of them over the course of a week, so you can prepare to receive what's to come.

Create your own spiritual routine. Tell yourself, "Every Sunday, I'm going to cleanse." This is going to make it so that you're living a magical life and not moving out of necessity.

It is really important to know what a cleansing may look like. Here's a brief experience from a client of mine:

I had a client who was very talented in her craft, but she didn't understand why she wasn't succeeding. I divined for her and did a reading, and I saw where her blockages were.

"There are things that need to be released, but you have to be ready. Are you ready?" I asked.

"Yes, Queen," she said, but my spirit said, "She ain't ready."

I did the ritual on her behalf anyway, and two-weeks later, she lost her husband…he didn't "die." They just broke up and ended up getting a divorce.

"Queen, me and my husband are no longer together. What's going on? I thought the cleansing was supposed to remove what's been holding me back?"

"He was the voice to the fear that told you your talent and products weren't good enough. *And,* he didn't use good moisturizer, which is why his knees were ashy." That was the biggest reason, in my opinion.

A couple weeks later, she got fired from her job.

"What's going on?" she cried.

"That job was holding you back from your product," I said.

After being stripped of what had been holding her back, she created a product line that became addictive all across the country. She continued to expand, excel, and exceed, but in order for that to have happened, she had to be ready. Certain things had to be removed first.

CLEANSING WORK

When conjuring Hoodoo and living in the actions of our ancestors, there were no measurements to anything. There were no formulas to doing spell work. We didn't even call it "spell work," so let's take that out of our vocabulary right now.

Whenever you are workin', do not get caught up with the number of drops or the specific materials you use because that will distract you from doing the actual work. It will take away from the asè.

Grandmama, Grand-mère, Grandpappy, didn't have a green candle; they had a fire pit. These details do not make the work. Everybody wants to be fancy nowadays, but that's not what workin' is about. It didn't take all that.

Another very specific point when pertaining to workin' is we did not have these new age titles: cord cutting, uploading, downloading, etc. We are not computers.

There are a lot of terms that we didn't use, and we did not have spell titles. I understand the reasoning behind them, but, traditionally, there were no spell titles. But, to make it easier to follow, I will give these workins' a title. Please, understand though that these are not *traditional* Hoodoo titles. We didn't have time to title anything. We had work to do.

Also, although, we suggest using Co. Meadows Conjure products, do not limit your magic/work to just these products. They are *not* mandatory. And, if you can't fix products yourself, you can always just use salt, water, pepper, and/or sugar—things that are very accessible.

Now, that we've discussed all that…let's get to work!

BRUSH/SWEEP YA' HOUSE
Broom Cleansing Spell

My family would say, "nettoyage de la maison" or "house cleanse," but "brush" or "sweep" is a term that is traditionally used when referring to a home cleansing.

This is because brooms in the African American tradition hold heavy weight in regard to our workins'. They can bring blessings in and send harm around. They are very powerful and shouldn't be played with.

Now, I've never flown on one, but that's something I'm workin' on. I'll make a *One-Minute Witch* video when I do.

Honestly, every single tool in Hoodoo has a dual purpose. The broom can bless or cause a mess. It just depends on how you use it.

Please note: The amounts listed are not carved in stone. Remember, if you don't have access to a particular item, you can always just use salt, water, pepper, and/or sugar in its place.

Things you'll need:

- A Broom *(It is better to use a broom with a wooden handle. You need materials that are bound by the earth.)*
- A Pot
- A Mop Bucket
- Water
- Co. Meadows Conjure Nettoyage (Cleansing) Oil
- Co. Meadows Conjure Bannir (Banishing) Oil
- 4 Lemons
- 4 Oranges
- ½ Cup of Rosemary

Directions:

1. Take the 4 lemons and oranges and cut them into halves.
2. Place them inside the pot.
3. Take the rosemary and place it inside the pot.
4. Fill the pot halfway with water.

5. Bring water to a light boil/simmer.
6. Then, slowly and carefully pour the water into the mop bucket.
7. Add 4 shakes of Cleansing Oil into the mop bucket.
8. Add 4 shakes of Banishing Oil into the mop bucket.
9. Take your broom and begin to dip the bristles into the hot water.
10. As you are dipping, repeat, "My house is cleansed. No weapons formed against my house will prosper. All negativity is removed."

    - If you are a person who is still struggling with disconnection from the church, then you may want to repeat *Psalm 51* and add hyssop to the water.

Note: This has nothing to do with your intention. This is you speaking words of conviction. This is not about feelings.

Giving words of conviction and the actions taken are important. Even if you said nothing, and you had no feelings there, the fact that you have gathered these spiritual allies together makes your action the work. It's how you act. It's what you do.

Here's a good example: when you sweep somebody's feet or place your purse on the ground, you have planted the seeds of the work without even realizing it.

To cleanse your house:

1. If you have a single-level house, you must sweep from the ceiling, down to the floor. You start in the back of your home—the back door or the back room.
2. Once you've done that, you are going to sweep from the back of the house to the front of the house. You do this all the way through.

Note: By using these fixed oils in your water, you don't have to say anything; you don't even have to do a lot of work. The oil does the work for you. Of course, you should bring your own energy into it too; that way, you'll see quicker results.

3. When you get done sweeping, pour the water onto your porch and sweep it to the front. This will repel all negativity and cause it to scatter.

If you live in an apartment:

1. Pour out some of the water. Wash your walkway/stairs.
2. Take that bucket and go to the river/crossroads. (Disposing when you are doing work is the most important thing. If you don't dispose, your doors are open for error.)

You don't necessarily have to do this full workin' every single week, but you should at least sweep from the back of the house to the front of the house.

CROSS ME NOT
Uncrossing Bath

An uncrossing bath is going to allow us to remove anything that has restricted us personally or deliberately by another individual.

Please note: I must make it clear again that the color of the candles used do not matter; however, if that helps you focus, then utilize colored candles. But, remember colored candles have no power in your workins'. Zero. This goes back to what we discussed earlier; it only holds you back from doing the work.

Things you'll need:

- 2 Candles *(can be black or white)*
- Co. Meadows Conjure Nettoyage (Cleansing) Bath Crystals *(or Epsom Salt)*
- Water
- A Soup Bowl
- 1 Egg *(DO NOT CRACK the egg)*

Directions:

1. Bring the water to a simmer.
2. Let it cool.
3. Place the water in a soup bowl.
4. Then, place the raw egg inside the bowl.
5. Take the water and fill your tub halfway. (Find a bucket you can stand in if you don't have a tub.)
6. Light the candles on either side of you, so when you get out, you're walking through them.
7. With the egg, rub it down your body and pray using *Psalms 51*.

DISCLAIMER: There are people who are adamant that the Bible has to be used in the traditions of Hoodoo in order for you to access *true* Hoodoo, but this is false and incorrect.

First and foremost, we could not read English. We were doing our magic on arrival with no Bible at all. However, once we were able to read English and were able to understand that these words held conviction, we began to use scripture. So, when you place a Bible on your ancestral altar, that highlights your ancestor's faith, not that you're workin' traditional Hoodoo.

8. Slowly wipe down your body, from head to toe. Do this 13x. Rub the egg over everything, even your lady garden or man parts. (As you're doing this, you're removing what has crossed you up.)
9. Once you've done it 13x, step out and air-dry.
10. Let the candles burn down. (You can use tea lights, chime candles, as these will burn quickly. If you do a 7-day candle, you gon' become an ancestor before the end of the cleanse.)
11. Once you've air dried, you can take your water to the river (it has to be running, moving water) and release it, or you can release it at a 4-way stop—in the middle of the crossroads.
12. Turn around and do not look back.

You can do this at night or in the morning. Once you do, you have been uncrossed. Doing this action will be doing the work.

HEALING CANDLE WORK

Fire Cleanse

This workin' is incredibly easy—so easy, it's ridiculous, but we think of it in a practical matter. It's a very practical healing work. If your child is sick, you can get them to do it too.

Things you'll need:

- Co. Meadows Conjure Guerison (Healing) Candle *(or you can use any 8-10-inch candle)*

Directions:

1. Take your candle and wipe it down your body, like you did with the egg.
2. Sit down in a chair (or somewhere sturdy).
3. Place the candle underneath your feet and roll it with your feet. (In essence, you'll be loading this candle with the ailments, illnesses, or pain you may have. All of this is being absorbed.)
4. Once you're done, burn it starting at sunset. (When doing fire work, let it be in a fireproof area.)
5. Burn it all the way down. (This is performing the action. As the candle burns away, so does the illness.)
6. Collect the wax and wrap it up in a brown bag.
7. Take it to the woods and bury it.
8. Once you bury it, leave and don't look back.

SMOKE DA HOUSE

Smoking Cleanse

This is traditionally the African American way of what people call today "smudging," but smudging is a ritual that is practiced by natives, not just the act.

For this workin', you can easily utilize Co. Meadows Conjure Fixed Incense, or you can make your own mix.

Things you'll need:

- Pine
- Rosemary
- Bay Leaf
- Frankincense
- Mustard Seeds

Directions:

1. Mix these items together and place on a charcoal burner with all the windows and doors closed. (Using frankincense heightens the mix and makes it more aggressive.)
2. Get the space full, then open the doors and windows.
3. Get your broom and sweep from the back to the front.
4. Once you have finished sweeping, throw mustard seeds out of the front and back door.

SMOKING SHEETS

1. Take a bath and clean yourself.
2. Once you've done this, you need to sit in a chair, air-dry, and place the hot charcoal with the pine, rosemary, bay leaf, and frankincense.
3. Put a sheet over yourself and allow the smoke to build up.
4. Once it burns out, throw the sheet off of you.
5. Take the sheet out of your front door and burn it. As you burn it, you burn away whatever issues you had.

GENERAL SPIRITUAL ALLIES

- Brooms
- Colognes
- Eggs
- Eucalyptus
- Hyssop

- Lemons
- Limes
- Nettle
- Oak
- Pine
- Rosemary
- Salts

CHAPTER 4
Love Work

Understanding where love work comes from is important. The binding workins' of yesterday are not the workins' of today.

Back then, our homes were being separated, and we were just trying to keep our families together; whereas today's love workins' surround more egotistical and narcissistic ways of thinking. It's about *your* benefit, and not *y'all's* benefit.

In no shape, form, or fashion should you believe that you have full authority over love. Love is an energy that is very abstract, but also very concrete, making it unpredictable. It can be unpredictable in the best and worst of ways. When doing love work, you should be cautious *and* conscious.

Back in the day, there were these obsession jars. *Love me, think about me, hold me, please me*...but what people don't understand is that instead of trying to get someone to be obsessed with you, become someone people can be obsessed with.

Also, it's important to point out that if you're doing love work on someone who doesn't belong to you, you are changing the natural order of things and going against that person's true will.

For example, a client of mine came to me and said, "Queen, I want this man, but this man has nothing to do with me. He focuses on nothing but his family. I want him to focus on just me."

It's safe to say that she was *thirsty* with a capital 'T'.

I said, "Let's divine."

After divining, it showed that they weren't meant to be. I told her the consequences, but she didn't care. So, I told her, "I will bind him to you, and he will become obsessed with you."

Once I finished the work, the man turned his attention on her and only her, so much so that 3-years later, she called back to reverse the spell.

"He is fixated on me."

"Well, that's what you wanted," I said.

"He stopped working and paying child support. Queen, everything that I wanted I got, but it was not what I needed."

Currently, I am in the midst of un-tying this situation. This man was truly unhappy but could not understand why.

It's important to remember that love work and sweetenin' work are different, so be careful who you bind yourself to. Do you have the ability to do so? Yes. But, just like you can, someone else can too.

Using the Color Red for Love Work

The color red traditionally does not represent love; it represents protection. It represents passion. Since I have brought up the space of color in this practice, let me say, the visualization of color in African and African American magic *was not* and *is not* an important factor to us. But, once the exploitation of our culture happened, these ideas were interjected into our culture. It became a selling agent; however, in some traditions, color does make a difference.

SWEETENIN' MOUTH WORK

This workin' is to encourage whoever is speaking bad on you that their words should be sweet. If you're workin' your own mouth, your target will only hear sweet things from your lips. This is great to use to dispel gossip and negative talk.

Things you'll need:

- 1 Orange
- A Petition Paper *(or personal concern) Please note:* Ideally, you'll need a person's personal concern, but if you don't have one, you can use a petition paper.
- A Personal Concern of Yours
- Co. Meadows Conjure Parlez Maintenant Oil
- 1 Vanilla Bean *(or a long string bean)*
- Sweetener *(honey, syrup, or sugar)*
- A Candle *(It can be white, which is universal, pink for love/romance, or blue for healing.)*
- A Bowl *(or Glass)* of Water
- Thread

Directions:

1. Starting at sunrise, light your candle, and put out your bowl of water.
2. Take the orange, carve a square in the top, and pluck it out. (There should be a hole inside.)
3. Anoint the bean with the Parlez Maintenant Oil.
4. Then, you are going to dress it with the sweetener.
5. Take the items (or petition paper) and wrap it around the bean using thread (or hair). If you do not have a personal concern, take the petition paper and write your name and your target's full name (or the two targets' names) on it.
6. Stuff the bean inside the orange and seal it with the plug.
7. Place the orange in front of your front door, or you can bury it in an ant bed and pour the sweetener over it.

Note: If you have a smart mouth or a slick tongue, you may put yourself in the orange so that your target will only hear sweet things on their ear.

8. Once you seal it, you are going to repeat, "May my lips be sweet, so are your ears." This will make it so that people will only hear sweet positive things even when you're struggling.

PINE BOWL
Reconciliation

This bowl is geared toward bringing healing and reconciliation to your relationship. It is a steady work. This means that it is always workin' as long as it's not retrieved.

Things you'll need:

- A Bowl
- A Pinecone *(closed)*
- Personal Concerns *(from you and your target or your 2 targets)*
- Co. Meadows Conjure Guerison (Healing) Oil
- Aluminum Foil
- Co. Meadows Conjure Guerison (Healing) Candle *(or a blue candle)*
- Thread

Directions:

1. Light the candle.
2. Take the pinecone and wrap the 2 personal concerns with it using the thread.
3. Place the pinecone in the bowl and drop 7 sprinkles of Healing Oil on it.
4. Repeat, "Our love is healed. We are healing."
5. Then, pour the water over it and say, "May our love be healed and purified."
6. Once you have done this, take the aluminum foil and wrap the bowl.
7. Lastly, place it under your bed, or you can bury it.

SUGAR BOWL

This particular workin' is very traditional and is geared toward sweetenin' whatever situation that is sour—a matter that is either romantic, professional, or personal. Whoever uses the sugar will be sweet to you.

Things you'll need:

- A Bag of Sugar
- A Container
- Personal Concerns *(from you and your target or your 2 targets)* or a Petition Paper
- Thread
- Co. Meadows Conjure Guerison (Healing) Oil
- Co. Meadows Conjure Venez a Moi (Love) Oil

Directions:

1. Tie your items together and place them in the bottom of the container that you're going to put your sugar in.
2. Anoint the bottom of the sugar bowl with the Healing and Love Oil.

3. Place the bowl in the location where it will be sitting.
4. Write the names of your targets on the petition paper and place it into the bowl (or add the personal concerns).
5. Pour the sugar into the container.
6. Place a little bit of the sugar on your tongue and speak the healing words that you need. Repeat, "You are as sweet to me as the sugar on my tongue."
7. The sugar will immediately begin to work and sweeten your situation.

Every time you use this sugar, you are workin' the sweetness, workin' the problem. Every time someone else (your target) is using it, they are being sweet to you. They are willingly fixing the problem. Crossing themselves up to sweeten the situation. Now, ain't that sweet?

TO ATTRACT A LOVER

Things you'll need:

- Personal Concerns *(yours and theirs)*

Directions:

1. Place those items together in your yard.
2. If a bird takes them away and builds a nest, you two will be together and build a home.

THOU SHALT NOT MOVE
Keep Your Lover in Place

This working is geared toward keeping your lover at home and keeping them faithful.

Things you'll need:

- Co. Meadows Conjure Contraindre (Compelling) Candle
- Co. Meadows Conjure La Maitrise (Mastery) Candle

- Co. Meadows Conjure Contraindre (Compelling) Oil
- Co. Meadows Conjure La Maitrise (Mastery) Oil
- A Bowl of Water
- The Soles of Your Target's Shoes
- Coriander
- Knotweed *(or Spanish Moss)*
- Ginger *(or Ginger Powder)*
- Thread

Directions:

1. Light both candles and put them opposite of each other.
2. Place the bowl in the middle and take the soles of the shoes and create the letter 'T'.
3. Then, take your right-hand, dip it in the bowl, and sprinkle the water over the soles 4x.
4. Next, anoint the soles with the oils. (Remember that when you are using fixed products, you don't have to say anything because the asè is already there. As long as you're doing the work, it will be effective.)
5. Put the Compelling Oil on the right sole of the shoe. You can speak, "You are where you belong. You belong to me. You cannot move; you will not move."
6. For the left side, use the Mastery Oil and say, "I demand that you stay put. I demand that you not move. I dominate your path."
7. Then, dress the soles with the ginger and coriander.
8. Fold the soles together and wrap them in any color thread.
9. After you wrap them, take some of the wax from one candle and pour it onto the soles.
10. Flip them over and then use the other candle.
11. Bury the soles in the backyard, facing the back of your property. This will keep your partner home and from running around.

PEACEFUL HOME SMOKE

Restoring Love & Peace to a Home

This particular smoking is conjured to achieve peace and reduce any scattered chaos in a home. It removes fogginess and negativity and implements understanding.

Things you'll need:

- Rosemary
- Pine
- 4 Lemons
- Co. Meadows Conjure Maison Paisible (Peaceful Home) Oil
- ½ cup of Sugar
- 1 tsp. of Mustard Seeds
- A Pot of Water

Directions:

1. Cut the lemons into 4s.
2. Place them in a pot of water.
3. Mix the sugar and mustard seeds together.
4. Grab a handful of rosemary (crushed rosemary is fine if you have it on hand, or you can purchase a rosemary bundle from www.conjuresouth.com).
5. Take a decent amount of pine needles and add it to the pot.
6. Then, add 7 drops of the Peaceful Home Oil.
7. Bring this to a boil and let it begin to steam until the water is gone. It will then begin to smoke.
8. Open your front door and throw everything outside.
9. Sprinkle the sugar and mustard seed out of your front and back door. (If there is anything left over, throw it away in your backyard.)
10. Finally, go to sleep and allow peace to fill your home.

SELF-LOVE BATH

This bath is designed to bring you self-love, self-confidence, self-value, and courage.

Things you'll need:

- Co. Meadows Conjure L'amour de Soi (Self-Love) Candle
- Co. Meadows Conjure Venez a Moi (Love) Oil
- Co. Meadows Conjure La Maitrise (Mastery) Oil
- 5 Oranges
- A Gallon of Milk
- A Bowl of Water
- Yarrow
- Allspice
- Bay Leaf

Directions:

1. First, burn your Self-Love Candle.
2. Then, fill the bathtub halfway with water (as warm as you can get it).
3. Pour the milk into the bathtub.
4. Add the oils.
5. Cut the oranges and then add the other ingredients.
6. Soak in the tub (in the morning) and bathe upward.
7. While you are bathing, you need to speak words of empowerment and conviction to yourself, words that reflect your worth.
8. Get out and allow yourself to air-dry.
9. Take a bowl and gather some of the bathwater.
10. Pour some on your front and back doorstep.
11. Lastly, allow the candles to burn as long as you are up.

LOVE ATTRACTION
Foot Track Workins'

This workin' is all about you leaving something of yours in your target's space and them leaving something in yours.

Things you'll need:

- The Foot Tracks/Personal Concern of Your Target *(Traditionally, this would be their foot tracks.)*

- Honey
- Co. Meadows Conjure Venez a Moi (Love) Dirt
- Co. Meadows Conjure Venez a Moi (Love) Oil
- Lodestone
- 4 Nails
- A Small Bottle of Sugar Water
- Dirt *(from your front yard)*

Now, let's get to steppin'.

Directions:

1. Gather dirt from your front yard.
2. If your target is a friend, or a friend-of-a-friend, and everyone is coming over, lay dirt outside of your front door. (Find a way to get your target to go outside, so you can collect their foot tracks. You can also go to where they parked their car and scoop up the dirt from there.)
3. Take the dirt from your yard and put it in its place.
4. Then, put their tracks in your front yard. Sprinkle the dirt from the walkway up to your front door.
5. Once you get to the front door, dig a little hole and put the rest of the dirt, honey, and lodestone there.
6. Before long, you are going to see the connection between you and this person become stronger and more intense.
7. Once you see the connection, sprinkle the sugar water on the spot 5x. (Do this once a month.)
8. Once your target comes over, throw the 4 nails out behind them, and that will lock them to your property.
9. Then, sprinkle the Love Oil 5x.

TO ATTRACT A LOVER #2
Return to Me

This is a very simple, very traditional workin'.

Directions:

1. Invite the person over. Once they come in and are having a good time, offer them something to drink (with the sugar from the Sugar Bowl).
2. Once they leave, sweep their foot tracks back to your house. (This will keep them coming back.)

FIX 'EE FOOD

Make a Person Hot for You

Things you'll need:

- Fresh Ginger Root
- Co. Meadows Conjure Venez a Moi (Love) Candle
- Co. Meadows Conjure Contraindre (Compelling) Oil

Directions:

1. Take the ginger root and rub it between your legs. As you rub it between your legs, say the name of the person you want hot for you.
2. Once the person comes over, cook with the ginger.
3. Light the Love Candle while you cook.
4. As soon as the person eats the food, they will instantly begin to desire you.
5. If you can't get the person to come over, take the ginger to the crossroads. Leave it there and don't look back.
6. If you want to get them in your bedroom, take the ginger root and dress it with the Compelling Oil and place it underneath your bed.

CHAPTER 5
Protection Work

Protection work is a very sensitive topic for me and should be for all people of color. The reason why this work should be the most utilized is the same reason why we used it 400-years ago.

Protection work is one of the first things I learned growing up, because it doesn't matter if abundance floods your life if your enemies come and take it from you, or if you're not here long enough to retain it. Let's get real. When it comes to traditional Hoodoo, it was meant to prevent the slave owners from raping men, women, and children. They didn't discriminate. It was also surrounded around not separating families.

One of the biggest things I encourage people to know is their customs. 400-years ago, we knew that if we split a tree, we would not return to that space again, so that's why we don't split poles today. Being binded was necessary because if we were ever separated, we would be able to find each other.

They hung us 200-years ago, and they're hanging us 200-years later. That is an ancestral space that cannot be ignored. Many other books about Hoodoo don't mention those things because they want to be inclusive, but our experience is *ex*clusive. That's why our magic is exclusive; it's *our* experience.

This piece is so important because a lot of people don't understand when I say that African American products should be produced by people of color who have the ability to conjure.

If you have recently seen an unarmed black man be shot or killed, and you don't know how important protection work is to you as a person-of-color, look to your son. This is the reality that he is living. We can say her name, "Sandra Bland." Look to your little girl.

For my non-people-of-color, if you feel some type of way about what is being done, or you know that it is wrong, thank you for your acknowledgment. But, please, understand that this acknowledgment does not grant you access to the experience. You will *never* have to fear for your life while walking to the mailbox or making sure that you choose the right clothes to wear.

Protection work can sometimes come across as being vengeful. For example, if I hang blue bottles in my yard, and someone crosses me, they will receive the curses of these spirits; it's not deliberate. These are just the consequences. It's not always about *creating* a barrier. Maybe, it's about repelling someone before they even come at all.

PROTECT YOUR HOME

Things you'll need:

- Mustard Seeds
- Co. Meadows Conjure Protection Candle
- Co. Meadows Conjure Protection Dirt
- A Sharp Tool *(ex: ax, hatchet, knife, spear, bow & arrow, scissors, etc.)*

Directions:

1. Begin by cleaning *and* cleansing your home.
2. Then, take the Protection Candle and light it at your back door.
3. Sprinkle a little of the Protection Dirt from the front to the back door.
4. Take the same dirt and sprinkle it in the 4 corners of the property.
5. Repeat, "My family is protected. My blessings are protected."
6. After making your rounds, go to the front door and toss out the mustard seeds.
7. Take the sharp object, facing outward, and stab the earth. This will protect you.
8. Once your candle burns all the way down, place the glass container in a bag, take a hammer, and smash it.
9. Bury the glass in your yard. (This will harm your enemies and keep them away.)

PROTECT MY PATH

Protect the Roads You Walk

Things you'll need:

- Bay Leaf *(one for each person you want to protect)*
- Co. Meadows Conjure Protection Oil
- The Right Shoe *(of every person you want to protect)*

Directions:

1. Anoint the bay leaves with the Protection Oil.
2. Then, put them under the soles of each shoe.
3. Lastly, anoint the bottom of the shoes by making an 'X' with the oil.

Your targets will be protected from spiritual and physical danger.

YOU SHALL NOT STAY
Hot Foot

The point of this workin' is to keep a person moving. This is something that enslaved people would do to keep the master moving, so that they didn't harm them or their children.

Things you'll need:

- Co. Meadows Conjure Hot Foot Dirt/Powder

Directions:

1. Take the dirt in your left hand, and at your front door, make 3 x's with the dirt. (Because this dirt is fixed, you don't have to add anything to it.)
2. But, if you know the target, and you don't want them at your home, write their name(s) on a petition paper and burn it to an ash. Add that to the fixed dirt before making the 3 x's. This will link any enemy to the workin', so they are not able to stay long or come to your property.

UNWANTED COMPANY

Repel Unwanted Company or Energy from a Home or Space

Things you'll need:

- A Broom
- Co. Meadows Conjure Repousser (Repelling) Oil
- Black Pepper

Directions:

1. First, you need to clean *and* cleanse your home.
2. Once your enemy comes over, you immediately sweep them out of the front door.
3. You are then going to anoint your broom bristles with the Repelling Oil and sprinkle the black pepper.
4. Then, you are going to turn the broom upside down with the bristles pointed to the ceiling. This will keep away the harmful intruders.

PSALMS 91

Things you'll need:

- Names *(of the people you want to protect)*
- Co. Meadows Conjure Protection Oil
- Co. Meadows Conjure Repousser (Repelling) Oil
- Co. Meadows Conjure Bannir (Banishing) Dirt
- Co. Meadows Conjure Protection Candle

Directions:

1. To do this working, you need to do it at the deepest/darkest part of night. (The latest you can stand it.)
2. When everyone else is asleep, light the Protection Candle at the front door.
3. While at the front door, write out *Psalms 91*.

4. Once you have it written, write everyone's name on the petition.
5. Take the Protection Oil and place it on the 4 corners of the petition and in the center.
6. Then, fold the paper towards you.
7. Next, bury this at your front door.
8. Make a circle with the Repelling Oil, counterclockwise. Then, you will make an 'X' on top of that space with the Banishing Dirt.
9. Allow your candle to burn all the way down.
10. You must pour the candle wax on this spot. Once you do this, don't look back. Just go to bed, hunny.

COVER THY HEAD
Protection from Spiritual Attacks

Covering the head has forever been an important aspect of African American spirituality; it is a custom. Playing in your hair, burning your hair, or throwing hair outside, for example, there are many traditions. The wisdom and asè comes from this space.

Your head can be protected in many different ways, but one way to protect it is to cover it. Using protection oils, repelling oils, clarity oils, and wrapping your head is very important.

You see it at the graveyard because possession doesn't look like Vodou or the Orisa in the Yoruba tradition. If you don't cover your head, you can react as a different person because another spirit has your head.

Church hats, head wraps, parasails, and umbrellas are all ways we used to cover up.

Always use an anointing oil to bless your covering. Your ancestors can come through rituals and sprinkle Florida Water or perfumes to protect you.

Things you'll need:

- Co. Meadows Conjure Protection Oil

Directions:

Take this oil and mix it with a hair oil or conditioner. Each day you use it, you are protecting your head. When you are in spiritual affairs, wrap your head with a scarf that has been anointed with the Protection Oil. (And always make sure that no one is touching your head, especially if they're sick.)

LAW KEEP AWAY

2020 Protests & Riots of Racial Injustice & Police Brutality

We are living in our ancestral days, so we must live in our ancestral ways. We have to live in the space of protection.

I'm not saying that we have to react to what's going on, but we must begin to live in this space. A lot of you are going to Kemet and Egypt…or you're jumping straight to the Orisa and Lwa. But you are skipping over the people who were in the Americas and conjured. Maybe, your great grandmama used to tell you to "put this in your pocket." Or, your grand-père said, "Take this packet and wear it around your neck."

These are the same ones who lit the lamps in the windows and went straight out into the streets during the Civil Rights Movement.

How did your ancestors thrive in the 40s and 50s? Not *survive,* but *thrive*? They were workers. Remember, prayer without works is dead.

Given what's going on in our country right now, we decided to include the following workins' for those who are protesting, or sitting at home, going out shopping, or whatever it may be. And, this is not just for you, it's also for your children.

Remember, we are doing *traditional* workins', not Michael's Magic Markers and Mojo Hands. Let's cut out all of the extra fluff and get to it.

Understand this, your first action of protection is your ancestors, so *feed* them. If you can't feed your ancestors and thank them for their supreme protection and guidance, nothing else matters.

HOW DO YOU FEED THEM?

The most important part is your time—giving them your undivided attention. Go to them and give appreciation for the times that they have already protected you.

And, you do not have to know your ancestors; they know you. You don't need pictures, Florida Water, crystals, stones, or incense. All you need is a bowl (or glass) of water and a candle.

REPEL YOUR ENEMIES

Things you'll need:

- Water *(from your ancestral space)*
- Black Pepper
- A Broom

Directions:

1. Take your bowl (or glass) of water and sprinkle it around your home.
2. Next, take a broom and throw black pepper on it. (As long as the bristles are upright, your enemies will be repelled.)

HEAD WASH/FLOOR WASH

Home/Personal Protection

Things you'll need:

- A Pot of Water
- Bay Leaves
- Mustard Seed

Directions:

1. Take the bay leaves and mustard seeds and bring them to a simmer.
2. Once cooled, rinse your hair with it and make sure to cover your head.

This same mixture can be used as a floor wash:

1. Using the bay leaf and mustard seed mixture, mop the floors in your house and/or your sidewalk.
2. When you are doing this, start outwards and sweep toward your home.

PROTECTION PATH

Things you'll need:

- Bay Leaf
- Basil
- *Psalms 91 (you can print it, write it out, or tear it out)*

Directions:

If you are going to be out in public, take your bay leaf and basil, fold it inside *Psalms 91,* and place it in your left shoe. This will protect your path as you walk.

CUT AWAY HARM FROM YOUR HOME

Things you'll need:

- A Knife or Scissors *(to cut away any harm to your home)*
- Oil
- Salt
- Black Pepper

Directions:

1. Anoint the blade away from you with the oil, speaking harm and illness away.
2. Then, bury it in your front yard, facing away from you. (Nothing will bring harm to you.)

WARNING OF DANGER

Things you'll need:

- Your Menstrual Blood
- 2 Bracelets *(1 for you, 1 for your child)*

Directions:

Women, if you are on your period, and you have children going out to protest, anoint a piece of jewelry, like a bracelet, for them and one for yourself. If the bracelet breaks, that gives you a warning. Call and check on them immediately.

CLOAKING WORK

If you're driving in a place that is high in violence and aggression, and you don't want to get caught up, use this workin'. This will get you out of sticky situations.

Things you'll need:

- 4 Pennies
- Slippery Elm
- Oil
- Black Pepper
- High John Root

Directions:

1. Create a mojo hand and anoint it with the oil.
2. Speak to High John, and say, "Please, allow me to get out of this."
3. Carry the mojo hand on you concealed. (Nobody can touch it, and make sure you feed it every time you are brought out of a sticky situation.)

BRING YOU STRENGTH

If you want to protest but don't feel very brave, or you're uneasy about something, use this workin'.

Things you'll need:

- High John Root
- Yarrow
- Star Anise
- A Bag

Directions:

Place these items inside the bag and secretly carry it on you. It will give you bravery.

BLIND THE LAW

Things you'll need:

- 4 Pennies
- Eyebright
- A Candle
- Salt
- A Bag

Directions:

1. Place all the items inside the bag.
2. Then, pour the wax inside. (This is going to blind the police from seeing you.)

REPELLANT WORKIN'

This is another space of repelling.

Things you'll need:

- Bay Leaf
- Mustard Seed

- Black Pepper

Directions:

Boil the items and pour the mixture around your property. It's a very strong repellant.

Note: In Hoodoo, Obeah, and Gris-gris, with salt, pepper, a bowl of water, and a candle, you can move mountains. Also, you can use salt for any herb that you don't have.

CHAPTER 6
Money & Luck Work

Regarding money and luck surrounding traditional Hoodoo, it is important to know that luck was more important than money because we needed favor on our side. We needed to take risks and not get caught. Money didn't matter because we didn't get payment anyway until we became free.

There are clear things you need to know surrounding luck when it comes to your head and your hair. Our luck, asè, and blessings are in our hair.

As a rule of thumb, don't let anybody touch your hair while you're gambling. They'll take your luck. And, be careful who you give money to. You're giving it to them from *your* pockets, so, in turn, they can control your pockets. A lot of people do not understand this.

Also, we lived our tradition; we did not practice our tradition. If it was using oil on our hands when we had to trade items, or having certain items buried at the front door so that we were walking with luck on our side, there was something that we did every day.

For example, how dollars face in my wallet, I am very cognizant that money has no choice but to come back to me. Or giving from my left-hand vs. my right-hand—left means that you're going to get it back, and right means that it was a gift.

What is money and luck truly about? Attraction. So, how do you amplify that attraction? Remember, when doing work, there's always duality. It falls under 2 categories—bringing things in and sending things out, attracting these conditions or repelling these conditions. When we're talking about these things, it's either this is what we want, or this is what we want to remove.

CAUTION: The next given content may result in fragile edges, possible perspiration, unconsciousness due to hitting the floor, and may cause other physical, spiritual, and/or mental harm.

Here is the real wig snatching wiggery of it all. We can put a lot of emphasis on the magic, but with all conjure, if you do not handle it on a mundane level, you are wasting your asè.

You can do money attraction work, but if you don't know how to make money work, you are wasting your asè.

When you do money attraction work, the asè you are granted may not give you all that you asked for at once, because your ancestors are going to give you what you're prepared for.

You're asking for $5,000, but you can't manage $500. And, since you can't handle the $500, they'll just give you $200.

When it comes to money, it flows to you. And, it can flow quickly, slowly, or steadily.

If you put out that you want a lot, it's your responsibility to handle it, or otherwise, you will not retain it. As the king or queen, if you pull the card of the *Crown,* you have to wear it. And, if you can't handle it, put the crown down, 'cause, babay, the crown does *not* make you royal.

Now, let's get to work and make sure your money ain't funny.

MONEY FLOW WASH

The ability to bring money into your home goes into foot tracking workins', depending on if you're using it in your house, front doorstep, porch, or sidewalk. This is also great for businesses.

Things you'll need:

- Co. Meadows Conjure Bonne Chance (Luck) Candle
- Co. Meadows Conjure Bonne Chance (Luck) Oil
- Co. Meadows Conjure Bonne Chance (Luck) Bath Crystals
- A Mop Bucket *(whoever you want to get the money have them spit into the bucket. If you don't want them to know about it, get a personal concern of theirs.)*
- A Broom
- Thyme
- Alfalfa
- Sugar

Directions:

1. Take the thyme, sugar, and alfalfa and place them into the mop bucket with hot water along with 7 shakes of the Luck Oil and 1 tbsp. of the Luck Bath Crystals. (You do not need a lot of herbs to do this. Truly, you only need as much as it takes to fit underneath your fingernail.)
2. Light the candle at the front door.
3. Speak into the water, "May my home be blessed, may those in my home be blessed." Repeat. (The spirits that you put into the water know that this is for financial responses. Remember that you are using fixed items.)
4. *Non-fixed items:* Repeat, "May my home have financial blessings, may those in my home have financial blessings."

If you have a walkway:

1. Sweep from the end of your walkway to the front door. As you're sweeping, you should speak, "My path flows with financial

blessings." (You don't have to say these words. You can just wish financial blessings to those on this path.)

2. If you do not have a walkway to your home, do this exact action, sweeping out your front door/porch.
3. Make sure that you pour the water out front.
4. If you live in an apartment, jar up the water and use it over the course of 9-weeks. Every day, do this action and light your candle.

SUMMONING QUICK LUCK OR BLESSINGS

Money Come to Me

The reason why I want to help you with this particular workin' is because we don't want to just focus on candles. A lot of work our people did didn't have much to do with candles at all. This workin' is using the space of incense.

Things you'll need:

- Co. Meadows Conjure Noir Chat (Black Cat) Loose Incense *(substitution: alfalfa, ginger root, and dried collard green leaf) Please Note:* This is not our recipe for Noir Chat
- A Charcoal Burner *(or firepit)*
- A Money Petition *(or a 6 of Diamonds playing card)*
- Co. Meadows Conjure Argent Rapide (Money) Candle

Directions:

1. Either using the incense (or mix), crush it up as fine of a powder as you can get it. (As you're mixing them up, you should be inviting the spirits for quick money.)
2. Place the candle at the front door and light it.
3. Place the *6 of Diamonds* (or the money petition) at the front door.
4. Bring the charcoal burner to the front door and put the incense on the burner. Let it burn away 4x.
5. Take the excess and sprinkle it on the front doorstep (or the sidewalk).

6. Once the charcoal has burned into an ash, place it on the front doorstep and sweep into your house.
7. Allow your candle to burn all the way down. This will summon money into your home.

MONEY SOAK

It is very important that you clean yourself prior to this workin', so that you are open to receiving financial blessings and luck.

Things you'll need:

- Co. Meadows Conjure Noir Chat (Black Cat) Bath Crystals
- Co. Meadows Conjure Bonne Chance (Luck) Bath Crystals
- Co. Meadows Conjure Van Van Bath Crystals *(substitution: use sugar and syrup)*
- 2 White Candles *(tea lights recommended)*
- 1 Cup of Honey
- 1 Gallon of Milk
- 1 Cup of Coconut Oil
- A Mason Jar

Directions:

1. Start at a half-hour. (ex. 9:30, 10:30, etc.)
2. Fill your tub with warm water, as hot as you can stand it.
3. For each bath crystal, make a cross from the back of the tub to the faucet, then from you across.
4. Then, pour in your milk, 1 cup of honey, and 1 cup of coconut oil.
5. Light the candles so that they create an entrance—one on the left-hand side and one on the right.
6. Step into the tub and pull this mixture up your body, up your face, into your hair, and understand, that you are covering yourself with luck.
7. Once you have done this 7x, sit in the tub, and allow yourself to soak for at least 30-minutes. Then, step out in between those candles and allow yourself to air-dry.
8. Next, collect the bath water and pour it in your backyard.

9. If the candles haven't burned down, take them to the backyard too.
10. Then, go to bed in white clothing. (*DO NOT* have sex or any kind of intimacy.)
11. The next day, wear bright and colorful clothing, and you will carry luck with you for a while.

FAVOR PACKET

This is great for granting favor to you, like loan approvals or promotions. It provides a space of mastery.

Things you'll need:

- High John Root
- Yarrow
- Solomon Seal Root
- A Personal Concern
- A Square Piece of Cloth *(doesn't matter the color)*
- A Piece of Thread
- Co. Meadows Conjure Moi Favor Oil
- Co. Meadows Conjure Contraindre (Compelling) Oil
- Co. Meadows Conjure La Maitrise (Mastery) Oil
- Co. Meadows Conjure Bonne Chance (Luck) Candle
- A Bowl of Water

Directions:

1. Light the candle next to the bowl of water.
2. Lay out your square piece of cloth.
3. You must give thanks to High John, the Conqueror for his diligent and everlasting work, and the success and work that he will bring to you. (It's important to honor this particular spirit.)
4. Place High John on top of the cloth.
5. Add your Yarrow, giving it thanks, as well as the Solomon Seal root.
6. Place the personal concern inside and tie the pieces together with the piece of thread. (Tie it in 7 knots or wrap it 7x.)

7. Once you have done this, anoint your packet 7x with each oil.
8. Carry the packet on you always when in this space.
9. If this is a workin' meant for you to dominate a person or place, put it in your left shoe when you're going to that place.

Note: This packet cannot be seen or touched by anyone but you. Otherwise, the asè will leave.

10. When you get your blessings, you must feed the spirits (at least once a month), anointing the packet 7x.

MONEY ON MY PATH

This workin' is very simple and very traditional. *Note:* You don't have to use the oils, but it only helps if you do.

Things you'll need:

- $21 ($20 + $1)—*Traditionally, it may have not been $21. It could've been a bag of coins, a bag of rice, or even cowry shells.*
- A Nail
- A Hammer
- Co. Meadows Bonne Chance (Luck) Oil

Directions:

1. Take the $21 and anoint the corners of each dollar with each oil.
2. Then, take the $21 with the faces facing you and nail them at your front door, behind a picture, on your front porch, or under your front doorstep.
3. Every so often, feed your money with the oil.

Note: This work allows you to enter into money and leave on a path to money.

If you want it to be specific, write the people's names on the money who you want to receive the workin'. You don't want people coming to your house to take from you.

CHAPTER 7
Divination Work

I grew up in a household for almost 20 years with 12 other people. I was able to witness the differences between divination, seership, spiritual abilities, and spiritual experiences. Growing up, we were not even able to read for guests and clients unless we had the anointing of seership. This is because the spiritual ability to see is different than divining.

In a space of traditional Hoodoo, the ability to be a seer or diviner does not make you a conjurer. Understand this, if a herd of cattle move uphill because they sense rain, does it mean that they are magical cows? No. It means that they have an *innate* ability. But, because they have this sense, it does not make them a unicorn.

SEERSHIP VS. DIVINATION

A *seer* has the psychic ability that gives you visions, dreams, and the supernatural and hypersensitive ability to know and to feel. This is an *anointed gift*—something you are born with. If you weren't born with this gift, you ain't gon' die with it. You can't develop something that you do not have.

Divination is the method of divining, or accessing divine knowledge and guidance from a divine source or space. This is *not* a gift.

Please, remember that a diviner *cannot* be a gifted seer, but a gifted seer *can* be a diviner, because divining is a method that *any*body can learn to do. As a diviner, you are not anointed with these spiritual gifts and abilities, but a seer who has this natural ability can learn to divine.

A *spiritual experience* is what you have with your ancestors. If you do not have the ability to clearly hear them, they have to communicate with you in a different way. This does not make you a psychic or medium.

DIVINATION METHODS

Traditionally, we did not have clair- this or clair- that. In the African American community, you had the "gift," and that was it. That term could have meant that you were a conjurer, a seer, or a healer. We did not have these fluff titles that you see today.

A lot of these titles have been created for monetary factors, but, traditionally, those things were not broken down like that.

Different gifts include:

- Hearing clearly
- Mediumship
- Necromancy
- Seeing Through Touch
- Clairvoyance
- Clairaudience
- Claircognizance
- Clairsentience

There are also many different *divination methods:*

- *Card Readings:* Tarot, Oracle, Playing Cards
- Pendulums
- *Gazing:* Water, Fire, Smoke
- Scrying
- Casting/Throwing Runes
- Casting/Throwing Bones
- Numerology
- Astrology
- I Ching
- Tea Leaf Reading
- Coffee Ground Reading
- Wax Reading

If you go to www.conjuresouth.com, we offer many divining methods.

One of the best ways to build your divination strength and guidance is to never *make* a decision. Divine on everything. I know this is going to seem very simple or juvenile, but this is how it works. Depending on your asè, your divination will grow differently. If you are the first diviner in your family, you are creating a lineage, so it's important to create this strong spiritual vocabulary. Having that and knowing what those definitions mean is easily done by divining. A beautiful foundation is created when you have a divination method. This is powerful because you're associating different meanings with different images.

If you have begun to create a sense of definition and understanding with these symbols and signs, you'll start dreaming with them.

For example, in your dream, you may be experiencing a lot of hardship, and then you see the '6 of Diamonds'. This could mean that you are going through some difficult financial things, but there is financial freedom, abilities, and resources in your path.

YOUR THIRD EYE & CHAKRAS

In the space of awakening your "third eye," this has to do with your psychic abilities. It allows you to tap into your higher self. But, unless you are a seer, it's not going to matter. You cannot have what you don't possess. You can't wake it up if you don't have it.

But, even if you're not tapped into that psychic ability, it does not mean that you can't divine.

To cut through confusion, use divination. In the space of traditional Hoodoo, Chakras are not magic; they deal with healing and are not traditional.

In this section, we are going to focus on traditional African American ways that we would divine.

ELEMENTAL DIVINATION

Each of us is primarily made up of an element, or we have an element that speaks to us most. We can connect with that element, and that element can provide us guidance.

FIRE DIVINATION

Fire Gazing/ Candle Divination

Fire divination is very simple to understand. Now, this is the way that I was taught, the way that I know. Understanding the language of the flame deals with your spiritual vocabulary. We are going to look at this in the space of candle magic within your work or veneration. Traditionally, we would see this in fire pits and lamps.

Also, understand that when we are talking about fire divination, we are solely looking at the flame, not the glass or the smoke.

- *Small, Weak Flame:* This flame is very close to the wick; it doesn't provide a lot of light. It defines weak workins'; things are not happening quick or strong enough. You shouldn't do it.

- *Standard, Steady Flame:* Comes clean off the wick. Communicates that your work is steady. There are no issues. If you are looking for a confirmation, this will give you a strong 'yes'.

- *Very High, Pointed Flame:* This flames comes *way* off the wick, possibly an inch, with a pointed tip. This workin' is communication that your work is gonna happen fast.

- *High, Strong Flame with a Pointed Tip and Black Soot:* This is weak. With black soot coming off, there is negativity surrounding the work.

- *Popping Flame:* A flame that is crackling, something or somebody is interfering in your work/plans.

- *Unlit Flame:* You can't light your fire. This work should *not* be done. You should do a cleansing before doing the work.

- *Explosive Fire/Untamed Fire:* This communicates destruction, that the spirits completely disagree. You have certain vibrations that are here to destroy you or the work that is being done.

In regard to Elemental Divination, we are focusing on candles and fire for now because it's the most commonly used and the most relevant. There will be other opportunities in the future to learn Water and Smoke Divination.

CARD DIVINATION

You can use tarot cards, oracle cards, or playing cards. In other types of card readings, we would have used playing cards.

Playing cards have been used all over the world in many different cultures, providing a variety of definitions depending on the one you are playing with.

My definitions come from different spaces, specifically, a traditional 1900s point-of-view. Spiritually, I was given strong definitions for these playing cards in the *Hoodoo Divination Cards* set, and they are an Alabama Gulf regional divining method.

Below are the definitions included in the *Hoodoo Divination Cards* set. You can find more definitions by ordering these cards and learning about the different spreads.

THE BASICS

Red Cards - Hearts & Diamonds

These cards symbolize and bring the message of 'Yes' as the answer to questions, in addition to being recognized as a good card or positive card. However, the red card could be something more, so be clear when you ask a question. Know what spread you are performing and be certain that you are reading either the *color only* or the *meaning of the cards*...but not both.

Black Cards - Clovers & Spades

These cards symbolize and bring the message of 'No' as the answer to 'Yes and No' questions. These cards are normally unpleasant but could be something more, so be clear when you ask a question. Know what spread you are performing and be certain that you are reading either the *color only* or the *meaning of the card*...but not both.

'Yes or No' Question (How To):

1. With the *Hoodoo Divination Cards,* always choose an odd number to perform a 'yes or no' question.
2. Only go by the color you draw; the meaning is pointless for a 'yes or no' question. You may confuse yourself by entertaining the meanings.
3. The lower the odd number of your choice is the quicker you will receive your answer with less confusion.

Yes, No, Maybe So!

- *All Red Cards (Hearts & Diamonds)* on 'yes and no' questions mean 100% 'yes,' or definitely a positive outcome without delays or holdups.

- *All Black Cards (Clovers & Spades)* on 'yes and no' questions mean 100% 'no,' or definitely a negative outcome.

- *More Red Cards than Black Cards* in a 'yes or no' question says, 'yes,' but there may be some delays or obstacles.

    ❖ In the *Hoodoo Divination Cards,* if there are delays, I normally read the meaning(s) of the black card to clarify the delay, if that information is sought.

- *More Black Cards than Red Cards* says, 'no,' but there's a little hope.

    ❖ In the *Hoodoo Divination Cards,* if there's a window of opportunity, I provide the meaning of the red card to express what the light at the end of the tunnel looks like.

Example: 2 Red Cards and 1 Black says, 'Yes' but with delays.

DIVINING MADE SIMPLE

At this point in your divining journey, we will focus less on the colors and more on the meaning of each card.

1. *The General Color Cast.* If you wanted to do a quick overlook of the matter you are presented with, just flip a number that speaks to you and read the colors as a general call…this is going to be good or rough depending on the answer. With this set, you would look towards the *Hearts & Diamonds* as the majority of good general outcomes, or the *Clovers & Spades* as a general call for a bad or less favorable outcome.

2. *4 Card Cast.* Read each card in conjunction to a timeline or stage in life with an ending result. For example, past, present, future; or early season, mid-season, and end of season.

3. *1 Card Cast.* As a general cast, this option helps you first learn the spirits of the deck and allows you to truly meditate on the exact message that you need to be aware of.

For more advanced playing card spreads, definitions, and meanings, please, go to: www.conjuresouth.com.

BONE READING

Sangoma Bone Reading is a Southeastern tradition, which originated in South Africa. In this space, diviners read both bones and charms. You have to go back into the space of ancestral lineage. Where you come from determines how you read, so it's important to understand different cultural spaces.

With seeds, nuts, shells, and charms, bone reading gives you the ability to receive divine messages, depending on the ancestral space. When you find something to add to your bone set that was placed in your path by your ancestors, its purpose is for you to recognize whatever that thing is. This is no different than driving or walking around and seeing '22,' '222,' '2222.'

What does this mean? These things hold a significance to you. That's why it is so important to build your spiritual vocabulary.

DIVINATION VS. SPIRITUAL GIFTS

Remember, divination is utilizing divining tools to get divine guidance. Having a spiritual gift is an anointing that you are born with, whether it's psychic-induced, conjure-induced, or healing-induced.

UNDERSTANDING YOUR BONE SET

In my bone set, I have a key that is turned, twisted, and warped, for example, which represents that there are roads that are closed. If I was going to the bank, and I came across this twisted key, it could mean that some of the roads to my finances are blocked.

What if it was a straight key? It would mean that my roads are open.

I also have a piece of knotted rope. This represents restriction. Now, take the straight key and the knotted rope. This would mean that your roads are restricted. Same as if it was the twisted key and the knotted rope.

DIVINATION MAT

Always have a potholder, a weaved mat, a soft piece of fabric, or a cushion to throw your bones onto. With my bone set, there are many different pieces, including some fragile pieces, like shells and glass, so I have to be careful.

And, yes, it's okay for other people to touch your bone set, but always keep it concealed to protect the energy of the bones. And, also, remember that how things fall matters. How things are presented matters.

HOW DO YOU CLEAN YOUR BONE SET?

Understand that bone reading is no different than any other divination tool. To clean your bones, you can just use water, but make sure that it is clean water. Unclean water will give you unclean messages. You can also use a little salt.

Directions:

1. Using water, you are going to douse your bone set.
2. You can also use Florida Water and douse your bone set 4x.
3. You'll want to say a prayer of cleansing. Speak clearance and clarity: "May these things be removed."

In Hoodoo, although, you have your smoking bundle, you can also use a loose herb incense.

1. Once lit, place the incense inside the bone set container and place your bones around it before putting the lid on top.
2. After letting it burn down for a while, take it outside and lift the lid 4x. (Whatever is on your bone set will be removed.)

Note: You can do a cleansing multiple ways, but always do it at the top of the hour for at least 30-minutes.

Also, if you have someone else throw for you, you should cleanse your bone set immediately. And, depending on how often you use them, you should cleanse your bone set at least once a month.

HOW TO READ YOUR BONES

Take a marker and create a big circle on your divination mat. Then, make a cross (+) within the circle. The cross represents *Spirit* (the vertical line) and *Earth* (the horizontal line). To achieve anything in this world, you need both.

If your bones land on the horizontal line, this is going to be a mundane matter, something earthly. If they land on the vertical line, this is going to be a spiritual matter.

Directions:

1. Draw a dollar sign ($) (in the upper left-hand quadrant), which represents *money and finances.*
2. Draw a heart (in the upper right-hand quadrant), which represents *emotions, heart, and love.*
3. Draw a circle with an 'X' inside (in the lower left-hand quadrant), which represents the *spiritual* (only sigils).
4. Draw a leaf or flower (in the lower right-hand quadrant), which represents your *health and physical well-being.*

CONJURE SOUTH
BONE READING MAT

In the next part, you have the space of the circles. The circles mean different things, depending on how you are reading. As you shake up your bones, you need to come from a clear space of what the question is.

GENERAL READING

Using a general reading, you are reading your *past, present,* and *future,* with you in the very center.

- *Inner Circle:* Past
- *Middle Circle:* Present
- *Outer Circle:* Future

CONJURE SOUTH
BONE READING MAT
DIAGRAM 1.2
FUTURE
PRESENT
PAST

WHAT SHOULD MY FOCUS BE?

This is good for a daily meditation.

- *Inner Circle:* 1st priority
- *Middle Circle:* 2nd priority
- *Outer Circle:* 3rd priority

CONJURE SOUTH
BONE READING MAT
$
LAST
SECOND
FIRST

CO. MEADOWS BONE SET

Pinecone: Healing and physical health

Cowry Shells: Upright *(represents male and 'yes')* and reverse *(represents female and 'no')*

Key: Doors are open/closed *(depending on how it falls)*

- *Facing away from you:* Closed
- *Facing towards you:* Open

Coin: Money matters; investments

- *Tails:* Negative
- *Heads:* Positive

Cayote Bone: Enemy; betrayal

Die: Risk and favor

- The numbers mean a timeframe. It could be days, weeks, months, or years. You have to be a seer to know which one, so if you don't know, don't read it.

Lovage Root: Love matters; emotions

4 Cowry Shells (All Males): Means 100% 'yes'

- If one is facedown, this means 'yes,' but there may be a delay.
- If 2 are facedown, it's 50-50.

4 Cowry Shells (All Females): Means 100% 'no'

- If one is upright, this means 'no,' but there's a slight chance or opportunity.
- If 2 are upright, it's 50-50.

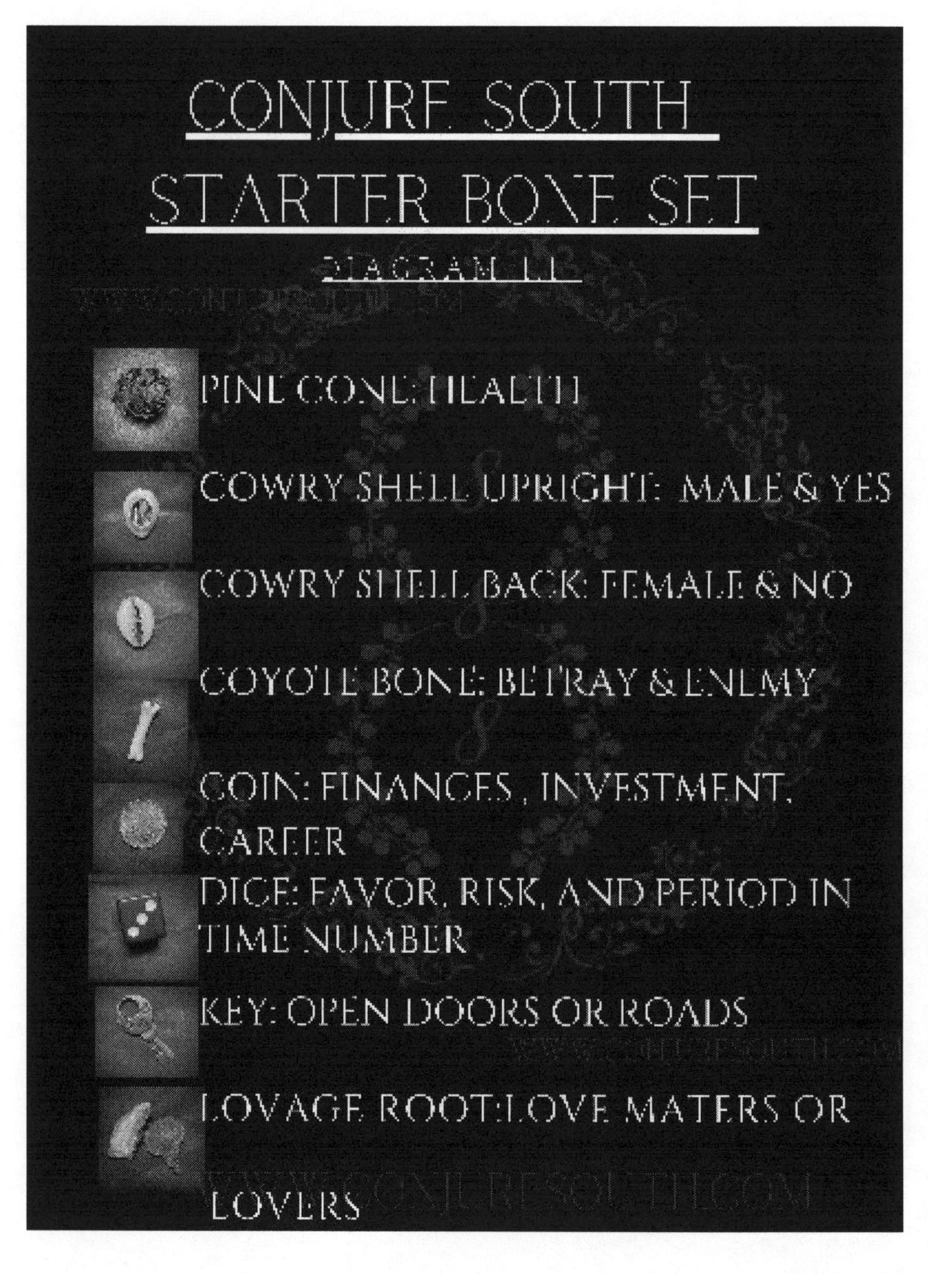

Note: When you do a cast and a piece falls off, you do not read that piece.

CONCLUSION

May the *Queen of Spades* provide you with the proper stepping-stone into the traditional ways of working African American conjure, root work, and divination. May this be the door that opens to you living your ancestral ways, or at least gaining a respect and educational point-of-view from our culture. Allow the *Queen of Spades* to be the voice for those who have not and were not able to speak.

Thank you for allowing the *Queen of Spades* to be the blueprint of traditional African American conjure and divination.

Made in the USA
Middletown, DE
24 April 2024